Fashions of a
Decade
The 1950s

Fashions of a Decade
The 1950s

Patricia Baker

CHELSEA HOUSE
PUBLISHERS
An imprint of Infobase Publishing

Chelsea House
An imprint of Infobase Publishing
132 West 31st Street
New York NY 10001

Library of Congress Cataloging-in-Publication Data
Baker, Patricia.
Fashions of a decade. The 1950s/Patricia Baker
    p. cm.
    Includes bibliographical references and index
    ISBN 0-8160-6721-X (alk. paper)
1. Clothing and dress—History—20th century—Juvenile literature. 2. Civilization, Modern—20th century—Juvenile literature. I. Title.
GT596.B32   2006
391—dc22   2006050142

Chelsea House books are available at special discounts when purchased in bulk quantities for businesses, associations, institutions, or sales promotions. Please call our Special Sales Department in New York at (212) 967-8800 or (800) 322-8755.

You can find Chelsea House on the World Wide Web at
http://www.chelseahouse.com

Author: Patricia Baker
Research for new edition: Kathy Elgin
Editor: Karen Taschek
Text design by Simon Borrough
Cover design by Dorothy M.Preston
Illustrations by Robert Price
Picture Research by Shelley Noronha

This new edition produced for Chelsea House by Bailey Publishing Associates Ltd.

Printed in China through Morris Press, Ltd.

Bang EJB 10 9 8 7 6 5 4 3 2 1

This book is printed on acid-free paper.

Contents

The 50s

January 1, 1950, was like any other New Year's Day. There was no change of direction on the political, economic, or fashion scenes to mark the start of the new decade. The election of World War II hero Dwight D. Eisenhower as president in 1952 was a milestone in a decade when many were looking back to the alliances and achievements of World War II as something solid to hold on to in a world newly split by East–West tension and the terrifying possibility of nuclear war. This conservative mood dominated the early years of the decade, both in the United States and in Europe, where conditions were quite different. America had emerged from the war years with increased prosperity. Wartime restrictions had been quickly removed, and the new "consumer society" was forging ahead, helped by such new developments as the start of the credit card system in 1950. But many European countries, Britain included, were still rebuilding their shattered economies, and there rationing continued well into the next decade.

These quite different conditions, however, produced the same effect on fashion—a veering away from the radical and extreme and a tendency to prefer the safe and normal. With the memory of the war still so fresh in many people's minds, "normal" felt good.

But the world was changing. The People's Republic had been established in China in 1949. India was enjoying the independence gained from Britain at the end of 1947. In Egypt, the year 1952 symbolized a new beginning with the departure of King Farouk, while the death of Joseph Stalin in 1953

▲Bathing beauties relax in swimsuits designed by Klein of Montreal: after the revealing early bikinis, these suits look quite conservative.

Exciting new colors to glorify your kitchen!

Frigidaire makes your life brighter—your daily chores lighter!

▲It wasn't unusual for family members and friends to gather in the house of whoever had a TV in order to watch a program of major interest.

▲The "exciting new colors" for the kitchen of the fifties were pastels—feminine shades, usually associated with bedroom or bathroom interiors.

A Forest of Aerials

Suddenly, television antennas were appearing on thousands of roofs. By 1954, one person in every seven in the United States had a TV set. Soon everyone was humming the commercial "jingles." Viewers on both sides of the Atlantic could watch the antics of Lucille Ball and Desi Arnaz in the *I Love Lucy* show, along with the neat packaging of singer Patti Page and the thrills of *Dragnet*.

COMMUNIST PARTY ORGANIZATION U.S.A.=FEB. 9,19.

▲Senator Joseph McCarthy points out the distribution of 250,000 Communist "fellow travelers" across the United States.

marked the end of an era for citizens of the Soviet Union. World War II had brought the end of the European colonial empires, and third world countries were striving toward economic development and political unity.

Although the war was over, the American government and military—and the general public—were becoming increasingly apprehensive about the extent of Communist influence in Asia and at home. Communism had to be contained, whether in the rice paddies of Korea or in the film studios of Hollywood. As a last resort, the thinking went, the nuclear bomb would deter the enemy, and the decade saw a number of political crises when everyone thought the bomb just might be used. Slowly, the realization of what this might mean began to spread: questioning of government and military policies began to gain ground, along with a cynicism among the young that would be the hallmark of the 1960s.

The McCarthy Hearings

Fears that Communists were attempting to undermine the American way of life were widespread in the early fifties, in what became known as the "Reds under the bed" scare. US senator Joseph McCarthy declared—but never substantiated his claims—that over 260 members of the State Department were Communist sympathizers or party members. A "witch hunt" and smear campaign began, with McCarthy heading the Senate Investigations Subcommittee of 1953. The televised hearings lasted for over a month, but even after they had been wound up, the allegations continued, ruining the lives and careers of hundreds of people. Between 3 and 5 million immigrants were said to be "subversive"; over 100 Hollywood film studio personnel were denounced, and 600 Protestant clergy were accused of being secret party members. In 1957, more than 700 organizations and publications were branded as Communist agencies.

▲Barbara Goalen, one of the most photographed models of the forties and fifties, is wearing a 1953 "Petunia" evening dress by Mattli. The extended shoulder detail emphasizes the pinched waist and echoes the wide, ballerina-length skirt.

Little Rock and Discrimination

Segregation in the American military and government services was officially ended in 1953, and one year later, the Supreme Court ordered schools to integrate pupils, whatever their race, "with all deliberate speed." Many southern states resisted this ruling for as long as possible, and in 1957, the governor of Arkansas used National Guard troops to ensure that no black students entered Central High School in Little Rock. His action resulted in federal troops being sent in to open the school to all students. By then, Dr. Martin Luther King, Jr., and others had initiated a number of boycotts against segregated buses, trains, parks, beaches, lunch counters, and diners.

▶Elizabeth Eckford tries to attend Central High School in Little Rock, Arkansas, in April 1957.

The Appliance of Science

The idea that science could control or even improve on nature seized the public's imagination. Chrome car fins that resemble rocket jets and the many designs based on chemical or atomic structures that appeared on household products and furnishings all show the fascination with science. Whether in the field of nuclear energy, the newly emerging computers, or the development of man-made substances such as nylon and plastic, science promised the answer to every problem. All the individual had to do was sit back and enjoy the fruits of hard work in the community and a contented family life.

That was the theory, but life wasn't quite like that for everyone. Many saw migration as the route to a better life. Puerto Ricans left for America's mainland cities, while migration from the Caribbean to Britain and France and from India and Pakistan to Britain also increased, introducing a substantial black population into these countries for the first time. Despite the bravery shown by members of nonwhite communities in World War II and later in Korea, racial discrimination was widespread.

Government responses to racial tensions were often hesitant and over-cautious, and increasingly communities began to take matters into their own

Scene by Cleveland Museum of Art   Lace Evening Gown by Hattie Carnegie   '56 Century—Four-Door Riviera-

Body by Fisher

Pioneers of today's newest and most thrilling advance in motorcar
the Four-Door Hardtop — as well as the wide-vision *Panoramic W*
and other famous Fisher Fashion Firsts found only on all GM cars

CHEVROLET   PONTIAC   OLDSMOBILE   BUICK   CAI

BODY by FISHER   GM GENERAL MOTORS

◀ Fifties style often meant a display of super-luxury, whether it was in the use of lots of shiny chrome on an automobile or a Hattie Carnegie designer gown of satin and lace.

▼The "dance at the gym" scene from the hit musical *West Side Story* reflects the kind of Saturday night entertainment enjoyed by most young people all over America. Suits for the boys and full skirts and high heels for the girls were the order of the day.

hands. The civil rights movement in the United States is just one example. And while black cultures had as yet made little impact on mainstream fashion, seeds were being sown that would bear fruit in the coming decades.

The Young Ones

Pop songs with titles like "White Sports Coat" and "Blue Suede Shoes" indicate the interest the young had in clothes, but for the most part, young people—in the fifties, this meant seventeen-to-twenty-five-year-olds—were expected to dress like their elders. Few retail outlets paid attention to them, although *Newsweek* in 1957 estimated that in the United States, young people probably had $9 billion of disposable income to spend. Women's magazines did tentatively raise the subject of young fashion but agreed that the difference in dress should be a matter of accent—"less sophisticated"—rather than actual styling.

So for girls, it was full skirts and stiff petticoats or, perhaps, a pencil-slim skirt and sweater. Tight-fitting pedal pushers or calf-length capri/pirate pants were popular leisure wear. Jeans (then called dungarees) became acceptable when Marilyn Monroe was photographed in them, and a particular fad of American girls was wearing a man's shirt outside their jeans. In high school, a twin sweater set or round, "Peter Pan" collar blouse were favored looks.

For formal events like weddings or school proms, young women still wore elaborate formal wear similar to that of their elders, but for the informal school dances, which formed many people's entertainment in the fifties, girls had more choice. Many favored very full skirts, some with deep, four-inch hems and often made of wool felt fabric, appliquéd with bright motifs, such as the ever popular

◄ Embroidered skirts were very popular. This full circle skirt in cotton broadcloth, with motifs evoking Venice and Paris, is paired with a simple three-quarter-length-sleeve top.

The Space Race

In the 1950s, it seemed that science had the answers to all problems. Nuclear power appeared to be a cheap, efficient, and clean source of energy, while the very threat of a thermonuclear bomb would persuade hostile nations to meet for peace talks. The discovery of the structure of DNA (deoxyribonucleic acid), the molecule that carries the body's genes, paved the way for important medical research. However, the one scientific development that took hold of everyone's imagination was the launching of the first space satellite. The successful Soviet firing of *Sputnik I* in October 1957, quickly followed by *Sputnik II* with Laika, a husky dog, aboard, shattered the confidence of western nations, which had assumed they were ahead in science and technology. The space race was on. The first, much publicized attempt by the United States to put a satellite into orbit in December failed, but by February 1958, the American *Explorer I* was orbiting the earth.

▶Debbie Reynolds was the embodiment of girl-next-door ordinariness, conjuring up images of white picket fences and soda fountains. This comforting image was important to America—and to the rest of the movie-watching world—in the postwar period.

◄ Rock-and-roll star Little Richard displays a little subversive dressing: well turned out in a linen suit, he has a striped shirt, no tie, and a T-shirt on display.

►The really wild one: Marlon Brando in T-shirt, jeans, and leather motorcycle jacket. The 1953 film, *The Wild One*, which represented society under threat from an alienated sector of its young people (*see page 56*), made antiheroes out of bikers and gave a huge boost to Brando's equally rebellious offscreen image. The T-shirt and the jacket—based on wartime flying jackets—indicate how the military clothing of the forties had been adapted into social wear for the next decade.

"poodle on a leash." A tight-fitting blouse tucked neatly into the skirt was usually anchored with a very wide, waist-cinching belt and flat-heeled shoes.

Young women took the floor to the Latin rhythms of the cha-cha, mambo, meringue or, increasingly, the new—and scandalous!—rock and roll.

For young men, it was shirt, tie, and carefully pressed trousers, unless you were rebelling against your family and society in general, that is. Then you rejected this conventional dress in favor of clothing that was darker, rougher in texture, and more crumpled in appearance or clearly exaggerated in styling. And people noticed.

A Man's World

As far as the family was concerned, the media message was that the male was the breadwinner, returning home to relax and perhaps do a few household repairs. He had unquestioningly obeyed orders in the war; now he obeyed the commands of big business. He dressed in a dark, quiet, understated manner for the workplace, but relaxed in slightly looser, more colorful clothing during leisure hours. As the decade progressed, jackets got longer, with the shoulders less padded, and the trousers narrower in the leg, although they were just as perfectly pressed. The introduction of new man-made fabrics brought a reduced weight of cloth and some experimentation in color and texture in the weave but no radical change in styling.

However, a revolution was taking place in the supply of clothing. Wartime garment production had resulted in increased efficiency, lower costs, and standardization of quality and sizes. Already, mass-produced men's shirts were available from chain stores. No wonder bespoke, or custom-made, garments

Elvis Presley

The phrase "rock and roll" was first heard in 1934, but in 1951, it was used to describe a brand-new type of American popular music that fused elements of gospel, rhythm and blues, country, and boogie. Five years later, Elvis Presley was its undisputed king, both in America and abroad, with such hits as "Blue Suede Shoes" and "All Shook Up." His stage performances seem rather tame by today's standards, but for many in the 1950s, they were outrageous, oozing with steamy masculine sexuality—so much so that when Elvis appeared on the popular *Ed Sullivan* TV show his hip gyrations were concealed from viewers.

◄ Two years after she had square-danced her way into the hearts of many North Americans, wearing a fashionably circular felt skirt, Princess Elizabeth was crowned queen of England on June 2, 1953. Like the first Queen Elizabeth, she came to the throne at an early age. Having given useful war service as an ambulance driver, she was now leaving behind her personal life to lead Britain from postwar austerity into what was billed as a "new Elizabethan age" of rebuilding, technological advance, and prosperity.

The Korean War (1950–53)

At the end of World War II, the East Asian country of Korea was divided along the 38th parallel into North and South Korea and occupied by Soviet and American forces respectively until 1948. Two years later, North Korean troops crossed the border to invade the south, capturing Seoul in three days. President Harry S. Truman immediately sent in American soldiers and called on the Allies for military assistance. After bitter fighting and great loss of life on all sides, the 38th parallel border was reestablished. However, this was not the end of American military action in the Far East. By the end of the decade, the US government had become involved in suppressing Communist guerrilla activities in South Vietnam.

►Rex Harrison's image as Professor Higgins in the smash-hit musical *My Fair Lady* matched his off-screen persona in the same way as Brando's, although this time the image was that of an English gentleman enjoying a relaxed country weekend. The cardigan was fast gaining ground as casual wear, along with sweaters and other knitwear.

were speedily giving way to ready-to-wear clothes. As retail menswear outlets showed steadily climbing profits, British and French fashion designers sat up and took notice.

There were other changes. Vests were becoming unfashionable, while men's cardigans, as worn by film star Rex Harrison, were slowly becoming acceptable at work. Hats, too, were losing popularity on both sides of the Atlantic, although they were featured frequently in advertisements and films. For the older generation, who still wore them, there were around seventeen different styles, one for every occasion. When it came to hairstyles, most men favored the

safe and rather military "short back and sides" with a side parting, slicked back with hair cream, although some young men were risking crew cuts, or cultivating a pompadour.

At the beginning of the decade, daytime leisure wear retained a rather military look, with a fitted sports jacket or navy double-breasted blazer with an ornate badge on the left breast pocket, worn with gray flannels or cavalry twill trousers. Increasingly, though, leisure wear began to mean a more colorful, open-necked sports shirt in drip-dry poplin, a comfortable sweater, and slip-on shoes.

▲Jacques Fath's stark colors and simple, structured shapes proved more popular in the United States than in his native France, but wherever it was worn, this outfit was definitely intended for the individualist. There is a hint of the ultra-sophisticated beatnik about it (*see pages 52–55*).

▶Nylons were back in circulation after the shortages of the forties. But the wonder fiber wasn't just for lingerie and stockings. As this advertisement indicates, it was now being used extensively in men's underwear, socks, and sportswear.

From the Cool to Hard Bop

Pop music of the fifties had few intellectual pretensions. If you were young and hip, your music had to be jazz—but what kind of jazz? *Jazz on a Summer's Day*, the film of the 1957 Newport Jazz Festival, displays the quality and variety of the fifties jazz scene, from the vocal art of Anita O'Day and Dinah Washington to the avant-garde style of Chico Hamilton and from the New Orleans tradition of Louis Armstrong through the gospel singing of Mahalia Jackson to the sophisticated rock and roll of Chuck Berry.

Elsewhere, Miles Davis was building on the reputation he had established in the late forties with a series of stunning small and large ensemble recordings made with the likes of Gil Evans, John Coltrane, Bill Evans, and Cannonball Adderley. Art Blakey's Jazz Messengers were emphasizing—thanks to Blakey's own explosive drumming—the beat of the bebop style and coming up with the more soulful and even danceable "hard bop" sound. And in the very last year of the decade, sax man Ornette Coleman released the first of a series of revolutionary, atonal "free jazz" recordings that were to reverberate right through the next decade.

▲Entertaining "the modern way." Everything about this interior, including the decor and the postures of the guests, hints at a lifestyle still described by many as "bohemian." Figure-hugging pants and shirt blouses were the order of the evening, and note that the outfit is completed by enormous earrings and matching finger- and toenails painted in a shade very far from the usual coral pink.

Fibers and Fabrics

The impact of the new artificial fabrics and fibers was felt mostly in underwear and leisure wear, although as early as 1952, haute couture designers like Christian Dior, Jacques Fath, Pierre Balmain, and the House of Lanvin had been featuring them in their designs. It was the practical qualities such fabrics offered —lightness combined with warmth, minimum shrinkage, quick drying, and waterproofing—that were exploited to the fullest extent in sportswear. The impact on underwear was in reduced weight, increased wearability, and easier laundering rather than in styling, which was, after all, governed by the shape of the outer garments. But man-made fibers had one other important impact, and that was on the color of clothing. When fabrics could be washed and dried almost overnight without fear of shrinkage, there was no reason why light and pastel shades couldn't be worn by everybody.

▶Society, however, was promoting dream homes and dream families. Mother—pretty in pink—and father are dressed for a big night out as soon as baby daughter is properly tucked into bed.

Woman, Wife, and Mother

According to the media, a woman's place was firmly in the home, and particularly in the kitchen. Women's magazines proclaimed that "femininity begins at home." The best career was marriage and raising a family: to remain unmarried meant one was "emotionally incompetent." For the many women who, in wartime, had enjoyed working outside the home and being in control of their own money, it was not an easy adjustment. By the end of the decade, social commentators had noted the increased use of sedatives and antidepressants and were talking about "trapped housewife syndrome."

Throughout the fifties, women's fashion, broadly based on Christian Dior's "New Look" of the late 1940s, promoted an idealized image of the happy housewife. The media continually used adjectives like "soft," "charming," and "feminine" to describe clothing, yet most fashion photographic images show tall, slender, heavily corseted models holding themselves in highly artificial, ballet-like poses, with little or no sign

The Cold War and Khrushchev

The Communist takeover of Czechoslovakia in 1948 and the blockade of the Western Allies' sections of Berlin did nothing to improve relations between Moscow and Washington. Even when control of Soviet affairs passed to Nikita Khrushchev on Stalin's death in 1953, tensions did not lessen. On the international stage, Khrushchev alternated between being the good guy and the bad guy. Although he tried, during his ten years of power, to improve the living standard of the average Soviet citizen, massive resources went to build up Soviet military power. Diplomatic crises continued throughout the decade, prompted by the sending of Soviet tanks into Hungary to suppress the national rising in November 1956, and by the attack by Britain and France on Egypt following its nationalization of the Suez Canal.

▲Scientists working on satellites for the exploration of space also had their minds on more immediate domestic problems. Orlon was just one of the many new fabrics designed for women whose lifestyle was speeding up by the day and who no longer had domestic help. "Plop it in the basin, pretty pleats and all," says the small print. "You can when it's wonderful, washable . . . winter-perfect jersey of Orlon."

The Suez Crisis

In the summer of 1956, worried by Egypt's increasingly close ties with the Soviet Union and Eastern Europe, the United States and Britain withdrew their offer of financial help for the building of the Aswan Dam in Upper Egypt. Because this project promised to transform the country's economic future, President Gamal Abdel Nasser reacted by immediately nationalizing the Suez Canal, explaining that canal dues would now go to finance the dam. The British and French governments—the major shareholders of the Suez Canal Company—began military attacks on Egypt that were widely and internationally condemned. The United Nations, backed by the United States and the USSR, insisted on a cease-fire, and a peacekeeping force was sent in. Both British and French diplomatic reputations suffered, while Egypt and many other Arab countries looked increasingly to the East Bloc for support.

overleaf: An overview of fifties fashion, as designers parade with their models against a typically opulent background. These are the "big twelve" members—significantly, all men—of the Incorporated Society of London Fashion Designers, including Hardy Amies, Mattli, John Cavanagh, and Victor Stiebel. The influence of Paris, and Dior in particular, can be clearly seen in this collection of evening gowns and day wear.

▲Bronwen Pugh, one of the famous fashion faces of the fifties. Her looks are typical of the cool, elegant, even haughty-looking models favored by photographers and designers at the time. Ironically, it was a style that made women look much older than their years and often indistinguishable from their mothers.

of emotion. No softness there! Few photographs showed the models in a work situation, outside, or in the home.

In fifties fashion illustrations for women, the relationship between waist and hips and between neck and shoulders becomes clear. A figure eight is repeated from head to toe, whether in garments from the fashion houses or from the discount stores—until 1957, when the loose-fitting styles of Hubert de

►For some, the New Look continued. In this outfit by Jacques Heim from 1956, this meant a three-quarter-length clutch coat, pearls, and a full skirt with narrow waist.

Givenchy, Cristobal Balenciaga, and Yves Saint Laurent for Dior heralded the new look of the 1960s.

For most people, though, all this was far removed from reality. The styles offered by the silver screen were not only more attractive, but, for once, perhaps more attainable. It was easier to identify with stars like Doris Day and Debbie Reynolds than with fashion models Bettina or Dorian Leigh. Even the sex symbols of the fifties were often photographed dressed like ordinary women, with Brigitte Bardot in gingham and Marilyn Monroe in jeans.

High Fashion

Fashion itself was moving slowly from select boutiques and the fashion runways of Paris, New York, Rome, and London into the better shops and the multiple chain stores. The format of display "islands," as found in self-service supermarkets, with their message of low prices and high quality, was increasingly adopted in clothes stores.

The days of custom-made, or bespoke, tailoring were drawing to a close. The mass-production processes introduced in wartime to fill bulk clothing orders now went into action to supply the new domestic demand. Cutters could now handle an amazing 200 layers of cloth at one time. Faced with the growing threat of ready-to-wear garment manufacturers offering standard sizes and all-around better quality, the fashion designers realized that future success—indeed survival—in a changed post-war society now lay outside their traditional clientele.

However, they wanted both types of customer. So, while quietly establishing commercial links with the mass-market garment suppliers and outlets in America and Britain, the Paris fashion houses decided to court

▼Screen sex goddess Marilyn Monroe and playwright Arthur Miller: the marriage the media simply couldn't believe. Here Miller's conservative and formal male evening dress is a backdrop for Monroe's glamour.

Marilyn Monroe

She was the sex goddess of the decade. Signed up by 20th Century Fox in 1946, it was some eight years before Marilyn Monroe (formerly Norma Jean Baker) hit the big time with the film *Gentlemen Prefer Blondes* (released in 1954), in which she worked alongside forties sex symbol Jane Russell. Although known for her figure, pouting mouth, and wiggle—said to have been deliberately engineered by having high heels of different heights—Marilyn also had considerable acting talent, as shown in *Bus Stop* (1956). Her marriage in 1958 to playwright Arthur Miller baffled the press, who could not imagine a love match between these two —brains and beauty being surely incompatible.

publicity. They began to promote the idea of "planned obsolescence," meaning that last season's wardrobe had to be discarded in favor of the new season's collection. This message was repeated twice a year at the spring and autumn shows, increasingly theatrical performances that attracted huge media attention. To further whet the public's appetite as well as to prevent their designs being copied immediately by mass manufacturers, fashion houses went to extreme lengths, banning cameras and sketchbooks from the shows. The feverish attempts of journalists to beat the system often attracted more attention than the actual collections.

Haute couture design became further and further removed from the real world, with the models presented as untouchable goddesses. But for the moment, the clothing industry still paid attention to the major fashion shows, taking one or two features from the collections and incorporating them into their garments. Soon, however, the pace of fashion would be set on the streets.

◀ Paris continued to dictate, but by 1955, the great Dior was moving into the longer look and a softened, sloping shoulder line.

Castro and Cuba

Fidel Castro, the lawyer son of a Cuban sugar planter, first attempted to overthrow the corrupt government of Cuba in 1953, but failed. After his release from prison, he fled to the United States and Mexico, returning secretly to Cuba in 1956 with about eighty supporters, including his brother Raul and Che Guevara. Moving from guerrilla tactics to a public rejection of President Fulgencio Batista's regime and all that it stood for, over a two-year period, Castro became a popular leader, giving voice to widespread discontent. The disturbances that followed his call for a general strike in April 1958 finally forced President Batista to flee in January 1959. Castro became prime minister a month later.

Hardy Amies adopts another Dior creation, the S Line. Note how the model's skirt has been pegged at the back to accentuate its cut.

Living Dolls

Housewife Life

From the end of World War II, there was a concerted move to persuade women to leave their wartime jobs and return to looking after the home. As leading American media adviser Ernst Dichter said: "We helped the housewife rediscover that homemaking is more creative than to compete with men."

Yet the usual media image of the housewife showed her not as a mother in comfortable pants and sweater but as a doll-like figure dressed in rustling, full

▲The ideal fifties woman was a homemaker, bringing up her daughter in her own image to yearn for domesticity. This is neatly underscored by the matching aprons, with their heart-shaped decoration.

◄ The *I Love Lucy* show, featuring real-life couple Lucille Ball and Desi Arnaz, entertained viewers throughout the fifties with the antics of a couple seen affectionately as Mr. and Mrs. Middle America. Every week, ditzy stay-at-home housewife Lucy plunged her household into chaos, to the frustration of her businessman husband, but usually managed to work things out in the end. Ironically, off screen, Lucille Ball was one of the most astute businesswomen in TV.

skirts, nipped waist, and narrow-fitting bodice. Even her apron had deep frills and a heart-shaped top and pockets.

The message was that a woman's catching and keeping her man depended not on her personality and mind but on her young, slim, hourglass appearance, her long legs precariously perched on high stiletto heels.

Working Women

If the housewife's role model was the Debbie Reynolds–style girl next door, the role model for the working woman was the character usually portrayed by Grace Kelly. Going into town called for a trim, closely fitting suit like the uniform of an airline stewardess, worn with high-heeled shoes. But there was little in this outfit of the power dressing of the eighties and nineties. Everything hinted at fragility, from the sloping shoulder line and the tailoring,

▲Two or more "cancan" petticoats of nylon net, often with frills in pastel colors, were worn under full skirts. These were stiffened by dipping in sugar solution and then drip drying.

▶The late forties New Look of Christian Dior still dominated fashion throughout the fifties. Button-through shirtwaists and skirt and blouse combinations, both with full skirts and slim-fitting bodices, were everywhere. High-heeled pumps were necessary to balance the effect but did not always prove the most comfortable casual wear.

which accented the curve of the bust, rib cage, hip, and pelvis, right down to the heels, which emphasized the ankle and calf. A little hat with face veil and feathers, gloves, and small handbag completed the picture.

Social life still retained some formality. For the more mature woman, theater going and even home entertaining called for cocktail wear (ballerina length) and evening wear (floor length). For young and old alike, this meant the romanticized image of the swan-necked, soft-shouldered female in rustling taffeta, shimmering silks (real or artificial), or layers of pastel nylon net decorated with lace, ribbons, and sequins.

▲Colorful prints on a white background were summer favorites, as well as pastel floral motifs. Like the high-heeled shoes, however, the tight-fitting bodices and narrow waists made few concessions to hot weather.

◄ Gingham, with its overtones of prairie style and girl-next-door simplicity, was a great fifties favorite on both sides of the Atlantic. This outfit, designed by Malcolm Brown, features the pedal pusher pants and the midriff-baring top introduced by Claire McCardell. The tops often featured a sash to be tied or buckled under the bust.

New Styles in New Fabrics

The new man-made fabrics brought exciting developments in sportswear, where fashion and function were equally important. American and Italian designers showed the way, producing lightweight but warm and easily cleaned sailing and ski jackets, based on wartime flying jackets, with nylon used for both padding and the main fabric. Zippers eliminated drafty openings. Two-way stretch fabrics were ideal for ski pants and motor scooter slacks, with instep straps to produce a smooth, tapered leg line and side zippers—front zippers were thought to be too provocative.

Swimwear also exploited man-made fibers. Elasticized two-way stretch fabrics were used in figure-controlling one-piece suits with preformed or padded cups to guarantee the best shaping. These suits, either strapless or with halter tops and frequently modeled on those worn by swimming star Esther Williams, were worn with extravagant bathing caps. The more daring two-piece bikini, launched by Parisian designer Louis Reard in 1946 after the atomic bomb test on Bikini Atoll, was gradually catching on. In America, there was another choice: the revolutionary softly draped stretch jersey suits of Claire McCardell, who continued to design simple but stylish easy-to-wear coordinates.

Color was everywhere, from the ski slope to the beach, with Italian designer Emilio Pucci in the forefront of European leisure wear. His loose-fitting, printed silk "scarf" blouses quickly became popular for holiday wear, while American women relaxed in tropical-patterned Hawaiian shirts and Bermuda shorts.

▲Like ice-skating champion Sonja Henie in the thirties, swimming star Esther Williams made a screen career out of her sporting abilities. She had a huge effect in popularizing the swimwear worn in her movies, although it was often extravagantly unsuited to practical wear.

▶The elegant styling of this black-and-white striped shirtwaist and the neat clutch bag mark the dress as town wear or even work wear for the still rare professional woman.

The Man in the Gray Flannel Suit

Corporation Man

Fifties man was much in demand at work, helping rebuild the economy, and also on the social scene. War had proved his bravery, endurance, and ability to obey orders. It was his turn to be waited on, after a day's work, by his wife, the homemaker. He didn't have to be fashionable—that was her job—but as the dependable breadwinner, his style of dress projected the image of a clean-cut, white-collar company man: sober, mature, and anonymous.

This was the "man in the gray flannel suit," the subject and title of a 1955 novel by Sloan Wilson. Such men could be seen by the thousands going to work every weekday morning, all dressed in their uniform of suit (usually single-breasted), white shirt, silk tie, and briefcase. Several fifties films played on the idea of the man in the gray flannel suit besides the one based on Wilson's novel, which starred Gregory Peck. In Alfred Hitchcock's *North by Northwest*, Cary Grant stars as a Madison Avenue advertising man accidentally caught up in Cold War espionage through mistaken identity. "Have you met our distinguished guest?" asks the chief villain, on capturing the hero. "He's certainly a well-tailored one," replies an accomplice. After a hair-raising adventure with a crop duster armed with a machine gun, Grant gets his suit dry-cleaned before confronting the villains and finally escaping death on the face of Mount Rushmore. He overcomes it all without changing his executive suit.

▼Hollywood's men in gray flannel suits: Cary Grant and James Mason star with ice maiden Eva Marie Saint in Alfred Hitchcock's 1959 thriller *North by Northwest*.

▼Casual suits were now acceptable dress not only for work but for many social occasions, providing the trousers had knife creases, the jacket fell well, and the shirt cuffs were just visible under the sleeve cuffs. Man-made fibers meant that the weight of the suits could be reduced by almost half. By the summer of 1957, jackets were longer and the line emphasized by softer shoulder padding and slim-cut lapels.

Ivy Leaguers

The gray flannel suit had also long been a favorite among the Ivy Leaguers, the college men of the long-established East Coast universities. The 1950s version was usually charcoal gray with a two- or three-button (widely spaced), single-breasted jacket, long and unwaisted, with narrow shoulders and one or no back vent. It was said to conceal the bulkier form of the American man. The English jacket was shorter and more fitted, usually with two back vents. By the mid fifties, the softer "Continental" shape favored on the west coast of America and in Europe emphasized a slimmer, longer line, from lapel and shoulder widths down to the more tapered trouser leg, now without the cuff.

The introduction of man-made fibers into men's suits marked American experiments in textures and color.

In 1951–52 there was a fashion for slubs—materials with "random" scattering of bright specks—and by 1955–56, synthetic silk-like suiting was popular, especially for the hotter months. Synthetic shirt fabrics meant shirts could be washed and drip-dried overnight. The shape of the collar was softening from long points, stiffened by celluloid tabs, to a shallow, rounded shape, with a screw pin or fabric tab placed behind the tie knot or buttoned down to the shirt front.

Another feature of Ivy League dress was the penny loafer. This was a comfortable slip-on, laceless shoe, with a strip or "apron" across the front and tongue. The name "penny loafer" came from the idea of sticking a shiny cent behind the decorated cutout shape of the apron.

▲American males led the way in enjoying the freedom of leisure wear, both in the loose fit and the vivid prints of sports shirts like this Hawaiian version popularized by Montgomery Clift.

◄ Pierre Cardin was one of the first French designers to create a fashion range for men. These three high-button styles were shown in February 1950: Montparnasse à la Flannel town suit with a Nehru collar (*left*); Saint Tropez summer suit of striped cotton, complete with a furled umbrella (*center*); and Toile, a town suit (*right*).

Leisure Time

The one area where the American male displayed his individuality was in leisure wear. Matching plaid or contrasting beachwear sets of boxer shorts or elastic-waisted trunks, matched with short-sleeved, loose-fitting cotton shirts or tops, worn open necked, were everywhere. More colorful still were Hawaiian shirts and Bermuda shorts, which were worn even by older men, like Presidents Truman and Eisenhower. War service in the Pacific and the entry of Hawaii into the Union in 1959 guaranteed the lasting appeal of these vividly colorful shirts, which had been popularized by Montgomery Clift in the 1954 film *From Here to Eternity*.

▲American men were more adventurous when choosing textured weaves for leisure suits, but the four-button sleeve-cuff and two-button, narrow-lapel jacket style still echo business suits.

An Artificial Freedom

Laundry Trouble

The media continually exhorted women to "wash whiter" as part of their wifely and motherly duty. Commercial laundries and dry cleaners weren't cheap, and anyway, dry cleaning removed the water-resistant finishes from garments until new processes were introduced in 1959. Laundromats were still few and far between, so once a week the boiler, washboard, and heavy mangle would be dragged out or—for those lucky enough to own one—the lumbering top-loader washing machine with integral mangle.

Suddenly, artificial fabrics came to the rescue. Some of them had been around for several years, but only in the 1950s was there large-scale production, dramatically increasing supply and lowering costs.

Nylon Revolution

Nylon—a by-product of petroleum pioneered by the DuPont company in the 1930s—was first used for women's stockings and lingerie, but during the war, most output went to supply the military demand for parachutes, ropes, and tires.

When American manufacturers were released from wartime restrictions, however, the demand for nylon hosiery was so high that the word *nylons* quickly replaced *stockings*. The advantages of nylon for underwear were considerable. Advertising promoted its qualities as easily washable, shrink proof, and quick drying, as well as lightweight and long lasting. "Goodbye to mending" was the message. It could be produced in all weights of fabric, from heavy fake fun furs to the sheerest of lingerie. It could feel as soft as silk, yet be stiff enough to hold out the circular skirts of a dance dress.

▼American housewives could now manage the home laundry in record time—and in top-to-toe elegance—thanks to the new top loader, but they still needed a man around to install it and fix the odd problem.

▶The easy-to-care for qualities of Orlon made it popular, particularly in knitwear.

▼Nylon stockings paired with nylon lingerie.

racle
time

...aculous fibres
...s Orlon," and
...sweaters are
...re, color and
...bility. They
...e softness.
...and vibrant,
...es that set the
...ts and business.
...no shrinking, no
...fading—and the
...rs are locked-in!
...resistant, too.
...ed, at most
...e stores.

Robert Bruce
ORLON SWEATERS

...CE INC. • 159 W. ALLEGHENY AVENUE • PHILADELPHIA 33, PA

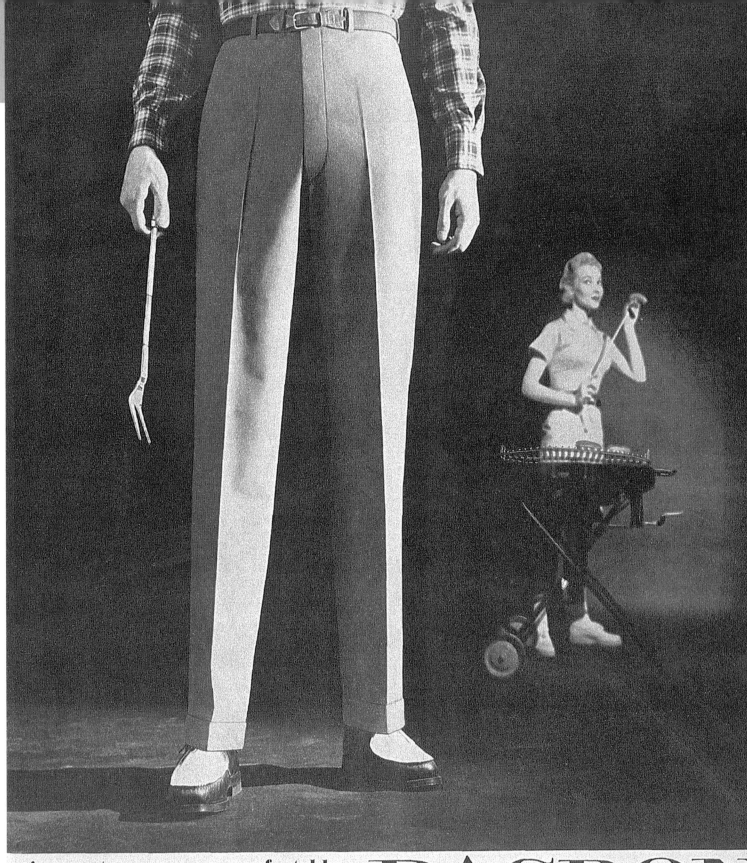

ou're neater ... **more comfortable**
... **with less care,** outdoors or in, when you wear
mmer slacks made with high percentages of "Dacron"* polyester
er. They keep you neat-looking longer with less trouble, even in
ggy weather, because "Dacron" holds off wrinkles while it holds
to its press. Cool slacks of "Dacron" are rugged, too, give you
eptionally long wear. See them in a variety of fabrics, styles, and
ors wherever you buy your better clothes.

◄ The 1956 movie *Baby Doll* spawned a fashion for shortie night wear, made from nylon or Tricel, based on that worn by the movie's star Carroll Baker, who portrayed a mixture of sex kitten and teenage Lolita.

Rayon and Beyond

Rayon was another low-cost, man-made fiber with a long history and a romantic, luxurious aura that was suggested by the name it was often given—"artificial silk" or "art silk." Few women realized it was made from wood pulp, with caustic soda for viscose and with cotton fibers and acetic acid for acetate.

By 1954, a by-product of petrochemicals, Terylene, or Dacron as it was first known in the United States, hit the headlines. A polyester fiber, it had first been developed in Britain before the war but then taken up by the American company DuPont. Like nylon, it was easily washed, quick drying, and shrink-proof, as salesmen in America demonstrated by diving into swimming pools or standing under showers fully clothed. Although crease resistant, it could take permanent pleating, removing at a stroke the tiresome chore of ironing. Lightweight but warm, a man's suit made of Dacron weighed only twelve ounces rather than the usual twenty, a boon in summer weather.

Suddenly the somber colors were gone, and shrinkage, moth damage (real problems in the past for knitwear), and ironing were virtually banished. All this should have given women more leisure time, but in fact, surveys at the end of the decade showed they were spending ten percent more time on household chores than in prior decades.

◄ Although the polyester fiber Dacron became widely available after 1954, it hardly revolutionized menswear styling. However, belts began to replace suspenders, and a closer fit without waist pleats became popular, even for leisure wear.

►The new artificial fibers made pastel shades and accordion pleats one of the most popular choices in the mid-fifties.

Haute Couture Heyday

Fashion Dreams from Dior

It was clear at the beginning of the decade that the fashion houses of the United States had failed to break the French designers' hold on haute couture. It was the runways of Paris that featured prominently twice a year in the glossy magazines of the fifties. Yet it was American designers who responded more directly to the needs of the contemporary woman.

The biggest showman of all was Christian Dior. He grabbed the headlines time and again, right up to his death in 1957. Dior promoted dreams. When his "New Look" was first shown in 1947, he remarked that "fashion comes from a dream, and the dream is an escape from reality." Dior also introduced the concept of planned obsolescence, maintaining that "novelty is trade." A new collection emerged from the House of Dior every six months, and with each spring and autumn collection, new "lines" were announced—the Oval Line, Princess Line, Sinuous Line, and Profile Line (1952); H Line (1954); A Line (1955); and Trapeze Line (1958, the brainchild of Yves Saint Laurent). Other fashion houses had little alternative but to follow.

However, many fashion commentators believe that Cristobal Balenciaga was the designer who really broke new ground. Spanish born, he was one of the few haute couturiers in Paris who knew how to cut: a master of technique as well as creativity. The tortoiseshell-like jacket back, three-quarter-length sleeves, slit vertical side pockets in skirts or patch pockets that showed below the suit jacket—all of these are said to be his innovations. Well before Dior's 1954 H Line, Balenciaga was releasing women from the highly artificial hourglass shape and adopting a more fluid functional line, while retaining the accepted "romantic" image for evening wear. This looser style was then further developed by his close associate, Givenchy, with his famous sack dress of 1957, which was in turn taken up and exploited to great effect by British designer Mary Quant and others in the early sixties.

▲One of the more unusual shorter styles featured an above-the-knee flounce caught into a tight hem or sometimes a band. Perhaps not surprisingly, the style did not prove popular because it was so difficult to walk in, but that did not deter determined followers of fashion.

WILL THE LADIES OBEY M. DIOR?

By ERNEST O. HAUSER

Christian Dior, tyrant of the hemlines, decrees short skirts for American women. This foxy French designer grosses $7,000,000 a year selling $300-to-$2400 gowns, and says, "Aren't people crazy to spend so much on a dress?" Can he bend the female world to his will again?

PHOTOGRAPHY BY EUGENE KAMMERMAN

▶The hot question of the moment: would American women obey the fashion "tyrant" in his decree that hemlines should rise?

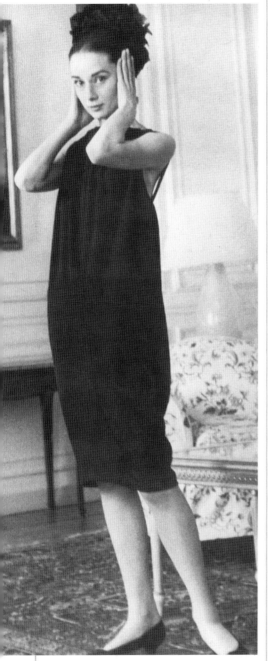

▲The simple, loose style of the sack dress was a direct challenge to the more common nipped-in waist of the mid-fifties and looked forward to the shift dress of the 1960s. One of the sack's attractions, apart from the freedom of movement it offered, was that it was easily dressed up or down with jewelry and accessories.

▲The tyrant himself—Christian Dior—surrounded by models wearing some of his evening dress designs in April 1950.

Givenchy and Chanel

The Givenchy "sack" took New York by storm, with American *Vogue* declaring in September 1957: "More than a fashion, it's actually a way of dressing." Anita Loos, writing in British *Vogue*, maintained that the loose fit of the sack lent mystery to the wearer. "I mean, no gentleman is ever going to puzzle his brain over the form of a girl in a bikini bathing suit."

Coco Chanel was the one Paris designer who designed wearable clothes for real women rather than promoting a fantasy image. She reopened her fashion house after a long postwar delay in February 1954, but the show got mixed reviews.

The Chanel look was unmistakable: the straight skirt (with or without box pleats) and the single-breasted cardigan jacket (with or without lapels) with braid or ribbon trims of contrasting color on the edges, hems, cuffs, and pockets, paired with a pussycat-bow blouse. Chanel's style was based on ease, comfort for the wearer, and practicality—as she maintained: "Fashion fades; only style remains the same."

American Innovation

American designers who had come into the limelight in the 1940s—Norman Norell, James Galanos, and Adrian—still remained influential. Mainbocher, so important during the war years, continued to accentuate the hips and waist: fitted, waist-length jackets and pencil skirts starred in his 1953 collection. He also initiated the craze for beaded evening sweaters and clearly enjoyed himself designing costumes for movies such as *Call Me Madam* (1950) and *Wonderful*

Town (1953). However, it was the easy, relaxed look of Claire McCardell's day and leisure designs in jersey, denim, and cottons that was to have the greatest and most long-lasting impact on American fashion, influencing both Bill Blass and Calvin Klein. Bonnie Cashin also responded to the needs of the fifties woman by bringing fashion and style into separates—a wartime invention to get around clothing scarcities—and so firmly established the idea of mix-and-match coordinates for the following decades.

▲A, S, and H lines: the three Paris silhouettes for autumn 1954. Hats are still very much *de rigueur*.

▼A Balenciaga coat from 1953, with three-quarter-length sleeves and slit side pockets. Loose, ample coats with interesting collars, made from textured fabrics—often mohair in the late fifties—provided a striking contrast to the close-fitting dress or suit worn underneath.

▲Fashions changed around it, but the Chanel suit, with its trademark braid trim, remained an unmistakable fashion classic throughout several decades.

The Undercover Story

Corsets and Curves

The unstated message of the decade was that female curves were all-important for catching and keeping a man. Young women in the fifties had to show that they were potentially good material for marriage and child bearing.

Until the last years of the decade, the hourglass line was smooth, soft, and so close fitting that it looked like a second skin. To achieve this, the body was squeezed and imprisoned in stiffly boned corsets. Dior may have announced that he was ending the encasing of women in iron, but his dresses could literally stand up on their own, supported by their internal boned structures.

If France was seen as the home of the fashion designer, America was seen as the source of the perfect corset. Many shop assistants acquired qualifications in corsetry since customers would frequently ask for a personal fitting. News of a "revolutionary" design in stock could result in the shop being besieged by thousands of women. Cages that crammed the body into the desired shape were given fanciful, frothy names like "Romance," "Merry Widow," and "Pink Champagne." Although lighter, more flexible plastic and celluloid "bones" eventually replaced the whalebone and steel stiffeners and the introduction of zippers meant much easier fastening, it must have been a relief to take off the foundation garment each evening.

Engineered for Uplift

Brassieres, either short or long line, called "Lovable" and "Sweet and Low," were similarly wired, particularly for wear with strapless and backless evening dresses. The cups were padded and fully stitched to give enhanced shape and cleavage, with advertising copy employing architectural terms like "uplift" and "cantilevered comfort." One widely advertised brand promoted the notion that its brassieres were such an integral part of dress that the customer might actually forget to put on the final top garment.

◄ Exceptions to the heavily girdled and corseted look were the designs of American Claire McCardell, famous for her casual jersey and denim garments. This 1950 beach outfit, doubling as swimsuit, displays the casual elegance typical of her designs.

►Halter-neck and strapless dresses with tight-fitting bodices required long-line strapless bras, which were wired and padded.

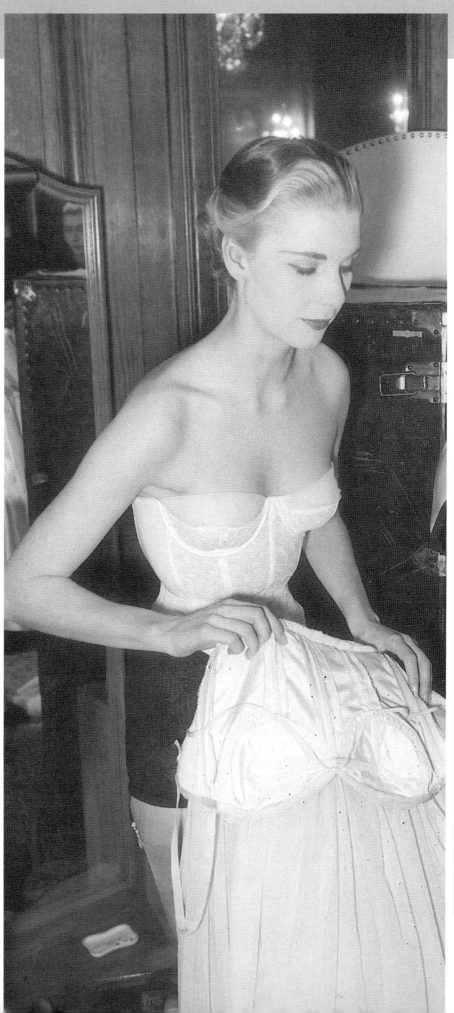

Heels and Hose

The final element in the armor was the stiletto heel. If the pencil-slim, full skirts emphasized the fragile hourglass figure, the stiletto drew attention to the ankle and calf and the movement of the hips in walking. Jordan of Paris was the first to combine steel with wood for heels in 1951, but the Italian shoe designer Ferragamo is usually credited with the invention of the steel support in a synthetic heel that allowed a very small heel tip. The impact was tremendous,

► A typical fifties face meant peaches-and-cream complexion, bright pink lipstick, eyes emphasized by liquid eyeliner, and penciled eyebrows. The look was completed by a neat beret-style hat and pearlized stud earrings: to have pierced ears was as yet unfashionable.

◄ Designers were getting into the accessories market in a big way. Cleverly promoting one fashion accessory on the back of another, this advertisement offers an Anne Fogarty scarf designed to match Cutex's "Pink TNT" lipstick.

►This design in corsetry promises "excellent abdominal support" from its "comfortable but firmly boned construction." The aim: an hourglass figure to fit Dior's wasp waist look.

HANDLE WITH CARE...
IT'S LOADED WITH LOVELINESS!

NEW "pink T.N.T."

FABULOUS OFFER
"PINK T.N.T." SCARF

designed by *Anne Fogarty*

Get the lovely PINK T.N.T. scarf shown here designed by Anne Fogarty! Imported pure silk crepe; 35 inches square; hand-rolled edges! Guaranteed $3 value, it's yours for $1 plus tab or card marked Scarf Offer from PINK T.N.T. lipstick or polish. Mail with name and address to Cutex, Box 110, N. 46, N. Y. In Canada: Cutex, Box 1171, Station "O," St. Laurent, Montreal. Allow weeks delivery. Expires Sept. 30, 1956.

Beautiful Dynamite for Lips and Fingertips

Gay as fireworks! Exciting as a carnival! "PINK T.N.T." is a radiant, rocketing new pink, sparked with a touch of blue. It's the hottest color that ever hit town . . . surefire ammunition for disarming your favorite masculine target! Get "PINK T.N.T." today and start the new season off with a beautiful bang!

NEW! CUTEX SATIN CLING LIPSTICK
Here's the new 24-hour-type lipstick by Cutex! Gives your lips round-the-clock color with no drying after-effect. **79¢.** SHEER LANOLIN LIPSTICK, **59¢.** For matching fingertips, chip-resistant CUTEX, longest wearing polish of all! Also, glamorous, iridescent PEARL CUTEX.

CUTEX
WORLD'S LARGEST SELLING MANICURE AIDS

▲Cosmetic pots still decorate the dressing table, but pan sticks, developed from movie makeup, were fast replacing loose powder and rouge.

not least on floors. Airline management and hoteliers met hurriedly to discuss how they might protect floors from the myriad indentations suddenly appearing.

By 1958, heels had gotten higher and the toe had become sharply pointed—the design of Beth Levine two years earlier, some say. Problems with posture and feet became common, and commentators drew analogies with traditional Chinese foot binding. However, many a young woman warded off unwelcome attention by "accidentally" bringing her heel down on an unsuspecting male foot!

By this time, nylon stockings were not only finer and much cheaper but had a better shape. Perhaps it was this closer fit that encouraged designers to raise hems from the lower calf in 1952 to an inch or so above the knee by 1958. With this shorter length came the "bare-legged" look of seamless nylons.

The lifting of postwar restrictions resulted in an explosion of interest in cosmetics, boosted by the entry into the market of movie makeup artists. Cheeks were gently rouged and eyes emphasized by liquid eyeliners, a little eye shadow, and masses of mascara. But it was the lips, women were told, that trapped a man, and most lipstick names implied cool seduction—into marriage, of course.

The face was framed by curls and gentle waves, carefully and painstakingly pinned up or pinched in clips before drying. Straight hair was definitely unfashionable except when pulled back into a chignon or French twist, but permanent waves, applied either in the hair salon or at home, solved the problem for those without natural curls.

▲Evening shoe, featuring metallic threads and stiletto heel, from footwear wizard Ferragamo.

►Clint Eastwood began his movie career as cowhand Rowdy Yates in *Rawhide*, one of the many westerns that filled 1950s TV screens and sent men running to the stores for plaid shirts and jeans.

◄ Singer and movie star Pat Boone was for many the personification of the clean-cut Ivy Leaguer: an all-American boy next door with button-down collar and plain blue jacket.

▼Shirley Jones as the girl next door in *April Love* (1958). Women's slacks had side fastenings, since front zippers were considered rather *risqué*.

Hollywood Dreams

The Silver Screen

Fewer people went to the movies than in the immediate postwar years, preferring to stay at home watching television or listening to the radio or record player, but for many, the weekly visit to the local drive-in movie was still important. On the silver screen, lavish productions and character stereotyping were the order of the day, with little of the experimentation to be found in contemporary theater productions. No one, argued Hollywood, wanted reality: the customer preferred pure escapism, thrills, spills, happiness ever after—and a role model.

Girl Next Door/Boy Next Door

The girl next door look was epitomized by Doris Day and Debbie Reynolds. The all-American girl was squeaky clean, tidy, and bubbling with health. She wore a full skirt, wide tight belt, and fitted blouse with a perky collar, white ankle socks, and penny loafers or saddle shoes and had her hair in a ponytail. The boy next door (also about twenty years old) was actually to be found on the college campus, wearing over his shirt a long cardigan or sports jacket and belted slacks or chinos (suspenders were definitely out). On his feet were easy-fitting penny loafers or white buckskin laced shoes, as popularized by singer Pat Boone. A bookish look and serious gaze, even horn-rimmed glasses, hinted at a certain vulnerability, which appealed to female moviegoers of all ages.

How the West Was Won

Throughout the 1950s, westerns were very popular. These tales of action and romance, of ruggedly handsome good guys and sullen-faced bad guys, offered welcome escape for the gray-suited businessman—and also confirmed the homemaking role of fifties woman, since even the independently minded film heroine would surrender thankfully into protective masculine arms in the final scene. No wonder many American men, in their leisure hours, shed their tailored jackets and trousers for fringed suede jackets, plaid shirts, and jeans, worn with moccasins or cowboy boots, like their movie heroes. As for women, the message was clear in *Calamity Jane*, where Doris Day only got her man once she had changed her cowboy clothing for gingham dresses. Calico, homespuns, lace, and crochet work became popular in a style based on Dior's New Look—but that was itself rather mid-nineteenth century in concept.

Cool and Sophisticated

This was the image every woman really yearned to achieve while elbow deep in the Monday washing suds. It spoke of good breeding, a comfortable income,

▲Doris Day projected her own brand of wholesome, unthreatening sexiness on screen and off. Here she wears the new stretch pants based on ski wear.

◄ The mid-forties look of Thelma Ritter's dress and shoes contrast with Grace Kelly's mid-fifties elegance in a scene from Hitchcock's *Rear Window* (1954).

sophisticated friends, and a household of servants. Stars like Margaret Lockwood, Deborah Kerr, Kay Kendall, Grace Kelly, and Kim Novak were walking, talking versions of the haughty, elegant models who graced the runways of the Parisian fashion houses. Their screen roles, however, made them seem more like "real" people. Perhaps, just perhaps, given the money and opportunity, one could be like them....

The Homewrecker

The pinup girl of the forties was still a potent image in the fifties. The embodiment of this was Jane Russell, one of the original forties "Sweater Girls," famous for her bosom and bee-stung lips. Her wardrobe was a mixture of girl next door and haute couture but more sexually inviting—a lower neckline, perhaps, or a more close-fitting dress. No ice-cool goddess this one: she was the girl you definitely didn't take home to meet Mother.

Equally famous were the cleavage of Elizabeth Taylor, the legs of Cyd Charisse, and the wiggle of Marilyn Monroe. Continental films cultivated a more aggressive, earthy image, and with it, a younger focus. Thus, from the "female tiger" role played by Silvana Mangano in the Italian film *Bitter Rice* developed the sex kitten, made famous by newly discovered French star Brigitte Bardot (*And God Created Woman*, 1956) and America's Carroll Baker (*Baby Doll*, 1956). Baker's scanty, short pajamas in that film, along with Bardot's gingham bikini and gingham wedding dress, immediately sparked off demands for similar styles in shopping malls country-wide.

▲Sultry temptress Jane Russell in classic sex goddess pose. Elegant sheath dresses like this one, shimmering with sequins, were the hallmark of American designer Norman Norell.

▶Fifties Hollywood was at its most lavish in the musical *High Society*, starring Grace Kelly as the ice-maiden daughter of a wealthy Philadelphia family. Bing Crosby and Frank Sinatra rounded out the starry cast.

Café Society

Crazy World

Not everyone in the fifties wanted to be associated with a gray flannel suit or a living doll image. The new decade had promised so much—World War II had been the "war to end all wars," or so one was told. But instead, as the decade progressed, the promises seemed to fade, with new political and military conflicts breaking out around the globe and the threat of nuclear weapons hanging over the world.

Relations between the West and the East Bloc were rapidly deteriorating, and in America, Senator McCarthy's witch hunts for so-called Communist sympathizers spread across all intellectual and cultural activities. The horizons of many young people were being widened through educational reforms, and on both sides of the Atlantic, the problem of racial discrimination could no longer be ignored.

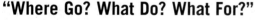

◀ Jazz was the music of the early fifties and the favorite of students and intellectuals. Racial discrimination may have been rife in society, but there was no denying that the leading exponents of jazz were predominantly African American. Miles Davis, Art Blakey, Thelonius Monk, Ray Charles, Milt Jackson, and Ornette Coleman were just a few of the many different interpreters of jazz style.

▶The young Brigitte Bardot was one of the few European actresses to achieve cult status in the United States. Taken up by the beat generation in their hunger for anything French, exotic, and sexy, she was already enjoying a high profile as a magazine celebrity and pinup when she starred in husband Roger Vadim's movie *And God Created Woman* in 1956. The movie, about an amoral teenager in a respectable small town, suited Bardot's teenage sexuality perfectly. "She is every man's idea of the girl he'd like to meet in Paris," declared one film critic.

"Where Go? What Do? What For?"

The nonconformists of the 1950s were the beatniks, whose philosophy was summed up in these three questions, put by Beat poet and novelist Jack Kerouac in 1958. Journalists first suggested in 1952, when the movement took off, that *beat* stood for "weariness" ("deadbeat"), but Kerouac corrected them, maintaining that his was "basically a religious generation" and "beat means beatitude, not beat up."

◀ A still from the movie of Jack Kerouac's sensational novel *The Subterraneans.* The movie was released in 1959.

The beat movement had similarities with the postwar existentialist movement, when students and intellectuals would meet in Parisian bistros to talk and argue over the latest writing of Albert Camus, Jean-Paul Sartre, and Simone de Beauvoir. From America's West Coast, ideas spread to New York's Greenwich Village, while Allen Ginsberg's protest poem *Howl* was heard as far afield as the jazz clubs and coffee bars of London.

Disquiet over established values was reflected in dress. The message was not just anti-establishment but anti-fashion. The clean-shaven look and neat hairstyle for men were out, as was the immaculately pressed gray flannel suit. Turtle- or polo-neck sweaters, preferably black, or a crumpled shirt and unpressed trousers, khaki pants, or jeans were in. As for the young beatnik woman, she dressed just as casually, in a black leotard, perhaps, or a long, heavy "sloppy Joe" sweater over a long black skirt and black tights. Occasionally, she wore tight-fitting straight-leg corduroy pants but always with flat-heeled ballet pumps. Black was definitely the color for the beatniks.

One Cappuccino, Please?

The focal point of all the activity was the coffeehouse, the favorite meeting place for real and would-be beatniks in the early fifties. Here one could listen to play or poetry readings and "cool" music, either on the jukebox or from a live jazz band. But mainly one could just hang out, lingering over a cup of cappuccino or espresso.

However, the impact of Italy was not confined to the import of Gaggia espresso machines and Italian pop songs such as "Che sera, sera" and "Volare." It was in leisure wear that Europe, and Italy in particular, was rapidly gaining an international name.

▲The looser, longer "sloppy Joe" sweaters of the late fifties were worn with tight pants, flat ballerina pumps, and strings of cheap glass or plastic poppet beads.

▼A publicity still from *Roman Holiday* (1953), in which over-protected princess Audrey Hepburn discovers freedom and romance in Rome from the back of a scooter. One of the hit films of the decade, it married the allure of continental Europe with the latest casual fashions—an irresistible combination for Americans.

From 1950 on, the Italian motor scooter manufacturers Lambretta and Vespa aimed their sales promotion at the European youth market, stressing freedom of the roads, friendship, and cheapness. As the scooter quickly became the "in" mode of transportation throughout Western Europe, it not only emancipated young Italian women, but also revolutionized their dress. Tight calf-length capri pants or pedal pushers or shorts were worn instead of full skirts, which could get caught in the wheels. Striped knit tops with dolman sleeves lent a continental air and gave freedom of movement, while a turtleneck sweater or neckerchief kept the drafts out. Hair was styled in a short gamine cut or kept in place with a headscarf, while slippers or flat ballet shoes were best for scooter riding.

Rebels Without a Cause

Antiheroes?

There were those who wanted to sit and talk about the state of the world and those who broke from established conventions by less intellectual methods. On the political scene, America's General Douglas MacArthur and Senator Joe McCarthy had won many supporters when they argued that action and retribution were better policies than diplomacy and compromise. On both sides of the Atlantic, violence and sudden death were featured in numerous films about World War II exploits, in detective novels about the adventures of lone-wolf private investigators like Mickey Spillane, and in TV police series like *Dragnet*. It seemed as if the best way to beat trouble was to stand alone and meet it head-on.

The Wild One

It was a short-lived reign of terror by a motorcycle club in a quiet California town sometime in 1947 or 1950 that grabbed the imagination of filmmaker Stanley Kramer. His 1953 film *The Wild One* starred Marlon Brando and Lee Marvin as two of a gang of violent bikers threatening an insular community. Their uniform and equipment spoke of the rejection and the undermining of accepted values—their powerful motorcycles were like those used by the highway patrol, the short flight jackets similar to those worn by World War II pilots and generals as well as US law enforcement officers. Black leather and blue jeans worn with T-shirts became identified in the public's mind with greasers, and eventually with the Hell's Angels.

The Right not to Conform

Two more American films were to grab the attention of the young. *On the Waterfront* (1954, again featuring Marlon Brando) showed one man in rebellion against authority and its ruthless exercise of power—in this case, gangland's hold over the docks.

◄ This man's crumpled, unpressed look is a compromise suggestive of someone not quite ready to trade in his tie and jacket for the black turtleneck of a beatnik.

▲James Dean and friends, in the new uniform of jeans, T-shirts, and leather jackets, confront authority in a scene from *Rebel Without a Cause*, one of the most controversial movies of 1955.

◄ The Teddy Boy was a peculiarly British phenomenon first seen in London's East End in 1952. Teddy Boys had no political or moral agenda: they just liked looking good, but that didn't come cheap—the suit alone could cost three or four weeks' pay. Thick-soled suede shoes, vivid Day-Glo socks, and narrow "drainpipe" trousers, sometimes with four-inch cuffs, were worn with a long, single-breasted, drape jacket with a single back vent, sloping padded shoulders, and velvet trim. Underneath went a flashy satin waistcoat over a white poplin shirt and shoestring tie. A carefully coiffed ducktail haircut and long sideburns were the final touches.

▼Jerry Lee Lewis was another of the unpredictable wild boys of the music scene who bridged the gap between country and rock 'n' roll, often leaping onto the piano and walking along the keyboard to stomp out a rhythm.

◀ Elvis Presley, king of the fifties. Once Bill Haley had let the rock 'n' roll genie out of the bottle, Elvis took the music to heights no one could have imagined, along with a stage routine that sent temperatures soaring.

In *Rebel Without a Cause* (1955), James Dean played a rootless, defiant teenager unable to communicate with parents who were themselves trapped in an unhappy marriage. With his tousled hair swept up and dressed in jeans, T-shirt, and jacket, Dean swiftly became the other great youth hero of fifties cinema, and his untimely death, in a car accident in October 1955, not surprisingly turned him into an international cult figure.

From now on, denim jackets, jeans, and plaid shirts worn without ties took on a whole new romantic aura.

Rockabilly

A cheap B movie of 1954 caused a storm both in the United States and Britain. *Blackboard Jungle*'s account of juvenile misbehavior and rowdiness was loathed by adults and loved by teenagers, who felt that Bill Haley's song "Rock Around the Clock" summed up their feelings: life is short, so let's enjoy it.

As for the audience, the boys sat in the usual adult tailored suit or leisure wear but with their hair in a slight pompadour and (sometimes blacked-in) sideburns, while the girls were in pencil-slim skirts and twin sweater sets or shirt-waisted dresses or full skirts and narrow-fitting blouses. Their hair was either drawn back in a ponytail or French twist or framed the face in waves and curls, while their lips glowed with lipstick in such shades as "Hound Dog Orange" and "Heartbreak Hotel Pink."

Chronology

News

1950 President Truman confirms H-bomb program.

1951 Juan Perón is reelected president of Argentina.

1952 Dwight D. Eisenhower becomes president of the United States.

1953 Queen Elizabeth II is crowned.
Stalin dies.
McCarthy Senate hearings open.
The U.S. military officially ends segregation.

1954 French forces are defeated at Dien Bien Phu, and French power in Vietnam ends.

1955 Civil rights movement begins with Montgomery bus boycott.

1956 The Suez crisis.
Elvis Presley arrives as an international star with the hit "Heartbreak Hotel."

Demonstrations take place in Little Rock, Arkansas.
1957 *Sputnik I* goes into orbit.

1958 Charles de Gaulle becomes French president.

1959 Castro overthrows the Batista regime in Cuba.

Events	Fashion
Credit card system is introduced in the United States. First-ever mass production of computers occurs.	Paris decrees that hemlines are sixteen inches off the ground. Emilio Pucci opens his fashion house.
Rock-and-roll era begins. First color TV broadcasts take place in the United States.	Balmain opens his ready-to-wear boutique in New York City. Balenciaga shows a waistless dress in his autumn collection.
Teddy Boys are sighted in London's East End.	British clothes rationing ends. Cavanagh and Stiebel open salons in London. Givenchy shows his first collection.
Mount Everest is climbed for the first time. James Baldwin publishes *Go Tell It on the Mountain*.	Bonnie Cashin opens her New York salon.
One person in seven has a TV set in the United States in contrast to one in twenty-four in Great Britain. Bill Haley appears in *Blackboard Jungle*.	Coco Chanel reopens her Paris fashion house. Designer Jacques Fath dies.
Sloane Wilson publishes his novel *Man in the Gray Flannel Suit*. James Dean dies in a car accident.	Mary Quant opens her boutique in London, with clothes aimed at those under twenty-five.
	First major Italian fashion show takes place in New York.
First meeting of the Channel Tunnel Company takes place in Britain. *West Side Story* opens on the New York stage.	In Paris, Dior is the only designer to show a waistline in his collection. He dies soon after. Givenchy shows the Sack.
Arthur Miller and Marilyn Monroe wed. Elvis Presley is drafted into the U.S. Army.	Yves St. Laurent introduces the Trapeze Line. Paris decrees that hems are above the knee.
The synthesizer appears as a new musical instrument.	St. Laurent revives the hobble skirt for the House of Dior. Suits from Mary Quant prefigure the styles of the 1960s.

Glossary

Amies, Hardy (1909–2003) British born, Amies became known for his tailored suits and lavish ball gowns, designed for ladies of the British aristocracy and the royal family.

Balenciaga, Cristobal (1895–1972) By the early 1930s, Balenciaga was Spain's leading fashion designer but moved to Paris in 1936. With his dramatic designs in strong, rich colors, he is believed by many fashion commentators to be the great innovator of the postwar period.

Balmain, Pierre (1914–82) French born, Balmain worked with Molyneux before opening his own salon in 1945. With a reputation for elegant tailoring, he quickly realized the sales potential of boutique accessories and the ready-to-wear market.

Bettina (Bettina Graziani) One of the top Paris models of the fifties, Bettina worked exclusively for Givenchy, who in turn named a full, ruffle-sleeve blouse in broderie anglaise (open embroidery on white linen) after her.

Cardin, Pierre (1922–93) Born in Italy but educated in France, Cardin became an established theater costume designer before moving into menswear. Having worked for Paquin, Schiaparelli, and Dior, he opened a salon in 1950, producing his first collection three years later.

Cashin, Bonnie (1915–2000) American born, Cashin began by designing for theater and films before working for sportswear manufacturers. She opened her own New York salon in 1953 and quickly became known for her clean, uncomplicated designs.

Cavanagh, John (1914–) Irish born, Cavanagh trained in London, Paris, and New York before joining Balmain's team in Paris in 1947. He returned to London in 1952 to open his own salon, retiring in 1974.

Chanel, (Gabrielle) Coco (1883–1971) An established French designer, Chanel reopened her salon in 1954 after World War II to a mixed reception since she rejected the New Look of Dior. However, by the early sixties, her functional designs had won new admirers.

Dior, Christian (1905–57) This French designer had instant success with his first collection, the Corolla Line (renamed the New Look), in 1947. He continued to exert great influence on the haute couture world until his death in 1957, by which time his salon had expanded into a multi-million-dollar fashion business.

Fath, Jacques (1912–54) Faith became established in Paris in 1937 but achieved worldwide fame after World War II for his witty and light touch. He was one of the first French designers to create for the ready-to-wear market in the early fifties.

Ferragamo, Salvatore (1898–1960) Born in Naples, Italy, Ferragamo moved to the West Coast of the United States in 1914, where he later worked in various film studios. Returning to Italy, he set up a shoe boutique in Florence and by 1957 had created 20,000 styles and registered 350 patents.

Givenchy, Hubert de (1927–) French born, Givenchy worked for Fath, Piguet, Lelong, and Schiaparelli before establishing his own fashion house. Acknowledged to be the creator of the sack dress, he enjoyed the challenge of designing for films.

Ivy Leaguers Students of East Coast colleges in the 1950s, Ivy Leaguers wore neat jackets and pressed trousers with white shirts with a button-down collar and tie. Female students dressed in twin sweater sets or Peter Pan collar blouses and sweaters, with pencil-slim or pleated skirts.

Jourdan, Charles An established shoemaker and designer before World War II, Jourdan opened a Paris boutique in 1957. He was quickly granted the Dior license to design and manufacture the footwear for that fashion house.

Mainbocher (Main Rousseau Bocher) (1891–1976) This American designer worked in London, Munich, and Paris. First a fashion artist and journalist, Mainbocher became editor of *Vogue* (French edition) and designed for Wallis Simpson, Duchess of Windsor, before retiring in 1971. His collection in 1939, before he returned to the United States, anticipated Dior's postwar New Look.

Mattli, Guiseppe (1907–82) Swiss born, Mattli worked in both London and Paris before opening his salon in London in 1934. In 1955, he ceased to design a couture collection.

McCardell, Claire (1905–58) An American designer, favoring a functional look in practical fabrics, McCardell is considered to have been one of the most influential designers in the United States for the modern career woman.

Norell, Norman (1900–72) American born, Norell became well known for his Hollywood and Broadway costume designs from the twenties, and his sequin-sheath evening dresses remained a firm favorite among American society circles for many years.

Pucci, Emilio (1914–92) A Neapolitan aristocrat by birth, Pucci was educated in the United States. His interest in sports led him to design some winter ski outfits that caught the attention of the fashion magazine *Harper's Bazaar*. He became the sports- and leisure-wear designer in the fifties.

St. Laurent, Yves (1936–) Born in Algeria, St. Laurent was employed by Dior in 1953 and took over on Dior's death in 1957, bringing the Trapeze Line and the "little girl look" to haute couture the following year.

Stiebel, Victor (1907–76) Born in South Africa, Stiebel first set up his salon in London in 1932, which closed at the outbreak of war. He reopened in 1952 and became a favorite designer for fashionable outfits for Ascot and other British horse races.

Further Reading

A great deal has been written and published about the 1950s—this reading list is only a very small selection. Magazines and movies of the period are another excellent source of information.

Adult General Reference Sources

Calasibetta, Charlotte, *Essential Terms of Fashion: A Collection of Definitions* (Fairchild, 1985).

Calasibetta, Charlotte, *Fairchild's Dictionary of Fashion*, 2nd ed. (Fairchild, 1988).

Cumming, Valerie, *Understanding Fashion History* (Chrysalis, 2004).

Gold, Annalee, *90 Years of Fashion* (Fairchild, 1990).

O'Hara, Georgina, *The Encyclopedia of Fashion* (Harry N. Abrams, 1986).

Olian, JoAnne, ed. *Everyday Fashions of the Fifties as Pictured in Sears Catalogs* (Dover, 2002).

Peacock, John, *Fashion Sourcebooks: The 1950s* (Thames & Hudson, 2000).

Peacock, John, *Men's Fashion: The Complete Sourcebook* (Thames & Hudson)

Peacock, John, *Fashion Accessories: The Complete 20th Century Sourcebook* (Thames & Hudson, 2000).

Skinner, Tina, *Fashionable Clothing from the Sears Catalogs* (Schiffer).

Trahey, Jane, ed., Harper's Bazaar: *100 Years of the American Female* (Random House, 1967).

Watson, Linda, *Twentieth–Century Fashion* (Firefly, 2004).

Young Adult Sources

Ruby, Jennifer, *The Nineteen Twenties & Nineteen Thirties,* "Costume in Context" series (David & Charles, 1989).

Wilcox, R. Turner, *Five Centuries of American Costume* (Scribner's, 1963).

Acknowledgments

The Publishers would like to thank the following for permission to reproduce illustrations: B.T. Batsford 15, 29r, 33, 37, 39b, 43l, 44, 46r, 47bl, 48t, 51b, 54r, 56, 58l; BFI Stills 32, 39t, 48b, 51t, 53, 54l, 57; Getty Images 9r, 14, 26t, 26b, 27l, 28r, 42, 45, 52; International Wool Secretariat 27r; Kobal Collection 13, 28l, 34t, 50l; Lighthorne Pictures 8, 18, 21, 23, 34b, 47tl, 58r; Popperfoto 6, 29l, 30r, 31b, 36, 41r, 24/25; Rex Features 11,12, 49, 50r; Topfoto 7b, 16, 17, 31t, 40t, 41l, 43r, 47r, 55, 59; Victoria & Albert Museum 30l; Vintage Magazine Co. 7t, 9l, 10, 19, 20, 22, 35, 38, 40b, 46l

Key: b=bottom, t=top, l=left, r=right

Index

Figures in *italics* refer to illustrations.